ISBN 978-1-330-41329-6
PIBN 10056804

This book is a reproduction of an important historical work. Forgotten Books uses
state-of-the-art technology to digitally reconstruct the work, preserving the original format
whilst repairing imperfections present in the aged copy. In rare cases, an imperfection in
the original, such as a blemish or missing page, may be replicated in our edition. We do,
however, repair the vast majority of imperfections successfully; any imperfections that
remain are intentionally left to preserve the state of such historical works.

1 MONTH OF
FREE
READING

at
www.ForgottenBooks.com

By purchasing this book you are eligible for one month membership to ForgottenBooks.com, giving you unlimited access to our entire collection of over 1,000,000 titles via our web site and mobile apps.

To claim your free month visit: www.forgottenbooks.com/free56804

English
Français
Deutsche
Italiano
Español
Português

www.forgottenbooks.com

Mythology Photography **Fiction**
Fishing Christianity **Art** Cooking
Essays Buddhism Freemasonry
Medicine **Biology** Music **Ancient
Egypt** Evolution Carpentry Physics
Dance Geology **Mathematics** Fitness
Shakespeare **Folklore** Yoga Marketing
Confidence Immortality Biographies
Poetry **Psychology** Witchcraft
Electronics Chemistry History **Law**
Accounting **Philosophy** Anthropology
Alchemy Drama Quantum Mechanics
Atheism Sexual Health **Ancient History**
Entrepreneurship Languages Sport
Paleontology Needlework Islam
Metaphysics Investment Archaeology
Parenting Statistics Criminology
Motivational

LITTLE BOOKS ON RELIGION

Edited by

W. ROBERTSON NICOLL, LL.D.

CHRISTIAN PERFECTION

WORKS BY THE SAME AUTHOR

THE CRUCIALITY OF THE CROSS. 5s.

THE PERSON AND PLACE OF JESUS CHRIST. 7s. 6d. net.

MISSIONS IN STATE AND CHURCH. 6s.

POSITIVE PREACHING AND MODERN MIND. 5s. net.

THE HOLY FATHER AND THE LIVING CHRIST. 1s. 6d.

RELIGION IN RECENT ART. 10s. net.

SOCIALISM, THE CHURCH AND THE POOR. 1s. net.

LONDON: HODDER AND STOUGHTON

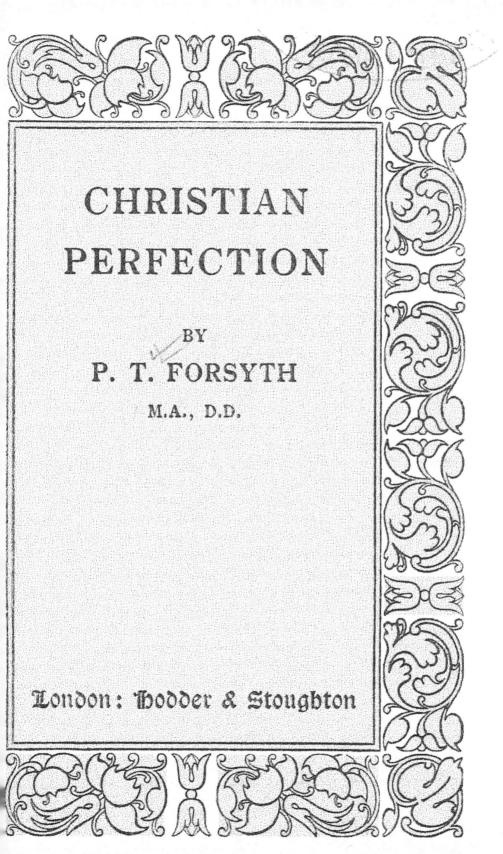

CHRISTIAN PERFECTION

BY

P. T. FORSYTH

M.A., D.D.

London: Hodder & Stoughton

CONTENTS

CONTENTS

'Whosoever abideth in Him sinneth not.
. . . Whosoever is born of God cannot sin.'
—1 JOHN iii. 6, 9.

THIS is one of the hard sayings which
are so fascinating in the Bible. It
raises one of the problems that are
so engaging to our moral thoughts,
and one of the anomalies that are so
irritating and depressing to our moral
experience.

Statements like these texts seem
to be met with every kind of
contradiction :—

1. In the first place, there is the
contradiction offered by John him-

A

self. 'If we say that we have no sin, we deceive ourselves, and the truth is not in us. If we confess our sins, He is faithful and just to forgive us our sins. If we say that we have not sinned, we make Him a liar.' We are to keep confessing, even as sons of God, which means that we keep sinning; for we cannot be urged to confess over and over sins we did before conversion, and which we had forgiven us as we entered on peace with God by faith. The children of God in John's own view keep sinning; yet here you have it, 'Whoso is born of God cannot sin.'

2. In the next place, there is the contradiction offered by our own experience. We know that we sin as surely as we know our life in Christ. As often as we confess Christ we have to confess him as Saviour and as Eternal Saviour. We

have to come as penitents. Our blessedness is always a salvation, not a mere donation. And we have new sins to confess since we last confessed His salvation and took His forgiveness. We cannot deny that we abide in Him; that would be to deny our faith altogether. But just as little can we deny our daily sin, that it is our fault if we are not more after His mind. If a Christian's sin means his severance from Christ, then the more Christian we feel the more severed we must be; because the more Christian we are in conscience the more sensitive we are to our sin, and therefore the less we must feel that we abide in Him and are born of Him, if this text have its face value.

And our own experience is only enlarged by what we know of the experience of greater saints than

ourselves. The history of holiness
is a record of self-abasements on
daily cause.   It is a story of triumph
and joy, but it is a daily humiliation
all the same, and a real, concrete
humiliation; not a vague and senti-
mental self-accusation, but a definite
self-indictment as the fruit of a
serious self-examination.

3. Moreover, texts like these seem
in contradiction with the very nature
of faith itself. We are told sometimes that it is faithless on our part
not to expect sinlessness in this life
from the power of God's grace,
deliverance entire not only from sin's
guilt but from sin's power, not only
from its power but even its presence.
But it is just the other way.   To
say 'I have now no sin' is to give
up that relation to God which is the
essence of faith, and to stand upon a
new and subtle kind of legalism.

The man who says that tries to enter
on a relation to God which is higher
than faith, and therefore he falls out
of faith. There is no higher relation
possible. Love is but faith in its
supreme and perfect form. It is the
impassioned expression on the face
of faith. There is but one attitude
of conformity to the will of God, and
that is faith: a faith that, being
itself an act of will and obedience,
always works outward into love. To
go beyond that is to step outside
the right relation to God. Faith is
not the mere sense of dependence
on God, but something much more
definite, positive, and real. It is the
sinner's trust in God the Redeemer.
Once a sinner always a sinner—in
this sense at least, that he who has
but once sinned can never be as if
he had never sinned. His very
blessedness to all eternity is a

different thing from the blessedness of the sinless. The man whose iniquity is not imputed is a very different being from the man whose iniquity was never committed. One sin is, in a sense, a sin in all. The whole nature is affected by it, and always. Pardon is not the cure of a passing illness, but a new birth in which the whole constitution is changed. It is not the dispersion of a cloud by the same sunny action as lights the ground. It was I who, at my will's centre, did that thing. It was my will and self that was put into it. My act was not the freak of some point on my circumference. It came from my centre. It was my unitary, indivisible self that was involved and is infected. Faith is the attitude of that same self and will of me to God. And as it has become a sinful self through me or my race of me's, therefore for ever faith is not the faith of the sinless but of the redeemed, not of the holy but of the sanctified, the faith and the love of those who have been forgiven much, forgiven often and long, forgiven always. The very nature of faith is trust of a Saviour, who is not the saviour of my past but of my soul; and it is trust for forgiveness, for forgiveness not only of the old life but of the new. That life is only what it is by reason of grace; and grace is not simple benediction, but blessing as the fruit of incessant forgiveness. It is the same forgiving grace that sanctifies us sinners in heaven and has mercy upon us on earth.

It is a fatal mistake to think of holiness as a possession which we have distinct from our faith, and conferred upon it. That is a Catholic idea

still saturating Protestant pietism,
and making a ready soil for the virus
of Rome and the plague of unethical
sacraments. Faith is the very highest
form of our dependence on God. We
never outgrow it. We refine it, but
we never transcend it. Whatever
other fruits of the Spirit we show,
they grow upon faith, and faith which
is in its nature repentance. Penitence, faith, sanctification, always co-
exist; they do not destroy and
succeed each other; they are phases
of the one process of God in the one
soul. It is untrue to think of holiness or sinlessness as a possession,
a quality, an experience of the soul,
and so distinct from a previous and
qualifying faith. There is no such
separate experience. Every Christian
experience is an experience of faith;
that is, it is an experience of what
we have not. Faith is always in

opposition to seeing, possessing, experiencing. A faith wholly experimental has its perils. It varies too much with our subjectivity. It is not our experience of holiness that makes us believe in the Holy Ghost. It is a matter of faith that we are God's children; there is plenty of experience in us against it. That we are justified and reborn is matter of faith. The spirit we have is no-possession of ours. It is God's Spirit, and it is ours by an act of faith. To claim sinlessness as the perfect state superseding faith is to fall from faith, not to rise from it. It is because we have sin that we believe—as belief must go in a religion whose nature is for ever revealed as Redemption. Our perfection is not to rival the. Perfect, but to trust Him. Our holiness is not a matter of imitation but of worship. Any sinlessness of

ours is the adoration of His. The
holiest have ever been so because
they dared not feel they were. Their
sanctity grew unconsciously from
their worship of His. All saw it
but themselves. The eye is the
beauty of the face because it sees
everything but itself; and if it
betray self-consciousness the charm
is dimmed. The height of sinlessness means the deepest sense of sin.
If we ever came to any such stage
as conscious sinlessness we should be
placing ourselves alongside Christ,
not at His feet. We should have
'life in ourselves,' with Him but not
through Him, or through Him only
historically. We should pass out of
faith into experience, or actual,
personal possession like our common
integrity. We should be self-sufficient.
We should cease to live on a constant
look to God in Christ, and repentance

would cease. We should be near the fall that so often comes to the sinless. We should be in the moral peril of those who, feeling they have attained this sinlessness, are ready to call each impulse good and lawful, as born from the Spirit with which they are now possessed. Moral perceptions are confused. Evil is called good because it is deduced from the Spirit. 'Out of a state of holiness can come no sin. I may do what I am moved to do and it is not sin.'

All this is contrary to the true nature of faith in a Saviour and His righteousness as the standing essence of the Christian life.

4. Perfection is not sinlessness. The 'perfect' in the New Testament are certainly not the sinless. And God, though He wills that we be perfect, has not appointed sinlessness as

His object with us in this world. His object is communion with us through faith. And sin must abide, even while it is being conquered, as an occasion for faith. Every defect of ours is a motive for faith. To cease to feel defect is to cease to trust. To cease to feel the root of sin would be to have one motive the less to cast us on God for keeping. Every need is there in order to rouse the need for God. And we need God chiefly, not as a means to an end, not to satisfy earthly need, to keep the world going, to comfort us, or to help us to the higher moral levels. We do not need God chiefly as a means even to our own holiness. But we need God for Himself. He Himself is the end. We need chiefly communion with Him; which is not confined to the perfectly holy but is open to all in faith, and possible along with cleaving sin. To treat a living person as an end, to seek him for himself, has but one meaning. It is to love him, to have our desire and energy rest in him, to have our personal finality in him. So it is that we need and seek God, not His help nor His gifts—even of sanctity, but Himself. His great object with us is not our sinlessness but our communion. 'Give me thy heart.' He does not offer us communion to make us holy; He makes us holy for the sake of communion.

It has pleased God to leave us *in* our sin (though not *to* our sin) that we may be driven to seek more than His help, namely Himself. We do not receive a new will, a new nature, from God, and then go on of ourselves, having got all that He can give. We are compelled by our cleaving sin to press on into close and permanent communion. 'My grace is thy sufficiency.' It is not simply our ability, but our sufficiency. It is our perfection no less than our power. We end with it as we began. We end with the same forgiving grace as started us. The recipients of grace are much more than the servants of uprightness. The prodigal was more after God's heart than his brother. And the same would have been true had the brother been sinless by a far finer standard than he had, so long as it was a sinless self-sufficiency, a self-contained sinlessness. The headlong sin is perhaps a safer thing than the sinless security. All life, it has been said, is the holding down of a dark, wild, elemental nature at our base, which is most useful, like steam under due pressure. So with sin and its mastery by faith. The pressure from below drives us to God, and the communion with God by faith keeps it always below. The outward pressure of nature, and even of perverted nature, in man develops in him through God a power which converts, controls, utilises, and exalts nature. It is doubtful if real holiness is quite possible to people who have no 'nature' in them, no passion, no flavour of the good brown earth. Take away that elemental rage from below and you make faith a blanched and inept thing. You have no more than quietist piety, passive religion, perfect in sound happy natures as an enjoyment, but very imperfect as a power. Faith, in the true sense, is all-sufficient, because it brings a rest which is itself power, force, will. It is the offspring of God's power and man's; it is not the mere occupation of man by God, which

as often means suppression as inspiration.

5. There is another aspect of the
collision between faith and the idea
of sinlessness as it is often pursued.
Sinlessness is a conception in its
nature negative and individual. It
has often been pointed out how for
this reason it tends continually to an
ascetic way of life and morals. Faith,
on the other hand, is in its nature
positive and social. Its spirit and
destiny is love. Love, and not sinlessness, is the maturity of faith.
There is an egoism about the sinless
idea which stamps this order of piety
immature, remote, purist, and pre-
occupied. Human fellowship is otiose
to it. Men can be done with or
without if only 'souls' be won. There
is a suspicion of want of heart. A
man may put away many sins, and
cultivate no small devotion, and yet

be a loveless self-seeker and a spiritual *aiguille*. There are certain forms of self-edification which run out into self-absorption, and leave men, and especially women, working at goodness rather than at duty. This is a frequent result of the culture of sinlessness, and it is in its nature antisocial. It becomes indifferent to churches, and finally to the Church. It is inter-denominational, then undenominational, then it ends in a new sect which is not a church so much as a coterie, and lives upon piety more than on faith.

But God's end in Christ is a Church community, apart from which and its faith and love there is no effectual sonship. In the design of God what is sinless is primarily the Church and not the individual. It is the Church and not the individual that is the counterpart of Christ. If we are complete in Christ, we are complete only in a holy and Catholic Church. A Church of sanctified egoisms would be no Church. Its essence would not be faith but moral or spiritual achievement. If the Church in heaven be one with the Church on earth its sanctity coexists with much sin. Its heavenly perfection is not sinlessness—'That they without us should not be made perfect.' Nor is any fancied sinlessness to which a mortal may attain to be disjoined from the sin of his age and kind. There is more of it in him than he knows. The isolation that he fancies is impossible. And the General Confession misbecomes him no more than it does the poor publican whose mood leaps to its words.

There may be much sin tarrying in a man if there be but the love of God overriding it, and the love of

man in God. Love is not a mere re-
duction of sin as an amount, but it
is a life turned in a new way, tuned
to a new key, vowed to a new Lord,
and lived in a new spirit. The difference (as I have urged) is one of
quality, not of quantity. And it is
along that qualitative way that our
perfection lies—in a heart that loves,
and loves not many but much. It
has the source of all its love in the
faith to which much is forgiven; the
source of its faith in the grace that
forgives much; and the condition of
its holiness in the fellowship of many
whose sin is still a sorrow but a sorrow
still. The holiness of Christ Himself
was a holiness conditioned by the
brotherhood of many sinners whom
He was not ashamed to call brethren.
And it is the holiness of One who is
organically united with a Church in
large part sinful still.

So much for the contradictions involved by the idea of mere sinlessness, especially for this life, as the form of perfection and holiness.

6. Where does the solution of these contradictions lie? We ought to find it in the same John who presents the problem. A real revelation, and a true apostle of revelation, push forward no problem whose solution they do not carry in the rear. The problem is but the deflection of the light as it enters our denser air.

John himself believes in two kinds of sin, and both of them are possible to the believer. 'There is a sin unto death . . . and there is a sin not unto death' (1 John v. 16, 17). It was a distinction current in the Old Testament, and it explains much in the New, where it is deepened. The sin unto death is when a man falls entirely out of communion with God. He loses the life of God from his soul permanently—I do not say eternally. He has not Eternal Life *abiding* in him. The world conquers him. The habit of his mind becomes earthly; and if he has relapsed it is a more inveterate worldliness that holds him, because his faithlessness makes his old faith seem a mockery. He is bitter because he is disillusioned. Sin becomes not an attack, an episode, or a lapse, but the principle of his life. I do not mean gross sin, necessarily, but the godless habit. It settles down on him and into him as frost penetrates the ground. He relapses, never to rise again. That is the sin unto death. And the sin not unto death is every transgression which still leaves the habit and sympathy of the soul for God a living thing. There are lapses which a man by vigilance, repentance, prayer, and well-doing can repair. Sin is a region he may visit, but it does not become his element. He falls into sin, but not into godlessness. The chill is thrown off. The frost does not go in upon him. The attack does not reach the heart. Every believer has more or less of this sin in him, and the risk of it always. But it does not cut him off from the divine life. There is a daily confession, a daily forgiveness, a daily cleansing of the channels of the grace of God.

Now the former, the sin unto death, is sin by pre-eminence. The man becomes identified with it. He loves sin, he does not love God. His life is one act of sin. And it is incompatible with the regenerate life of faith. Whoso is born of God sinneth not in this sense. No man so sinning abides in Christ. Whoso abides in Christ sinneth not this sin. He

may commit sins, but he does not live
sin like the man who has returned
to be a worldling and practically re-
nounced Christ. Sin does not become
his world, his element. His sympathies and affinities, his effort and his
service, are all to goodness and to
God. His life on the whole and at
the core is a life of faith and of growing mastery over the world.

7. But John seems to imply that
once a man is born of God relapse is
impossible: iii. 9, 'He cannot sin,
because he is born of God.' Now, I
admit with great reverence that for
the modern Christian mind such
language is too absolute. Had John
written with an eye to modern ways
of thinking he would have said something to show on the spot, as he does
show elsewhere, that he did know the
difference between the ideal and the
actual, between a moral and a natural

necessity, between a judgment of experience and a judgment of faith. If we reason from experience we do find that men born of God have fallen into sin, and have sinned even unto death. Men remain free, with the perils of freedom, even as the subjects of divine grace. The compulsions of God are not natural necessities. The 'cannot' here does not mean a natural impossibility as if we said, he cannot fly, cannot fall from the earth's surface, if he is born on the earth. There is no such necessity as if, when a man is born of God, all the rest followed of itself by inevitable sequence and a causative chain. It is not as if sinlessness then worked itself out in us without effort. To be born of God means to pass into fellowship with a living will; that is to say, it is to develop into a greater intensity of living will, to be more than ever a doer, a free doer, if we are like God, and a doer of righteousness, of holiness. 'Cannot sin' means not that he is not able to sin, but that his principle will not allow him to sin. As the regenerate personality he cannot do it. He may, of course, be at the same time something other than the regenerate personality in his actual condition so far. But in so far as he is the servant of that personality he cannot. 'You cannot do it,' we say to a man, not denying the physical possibility, as if he were paralysed or in jail, but denying the moral possibility. 'You cannot, consistently with your principles, do it; you cannot, with your nature, with all I have known of you, do it; it would not be you if you did it; you simply cannot.' Ideally, whoso is born of God cannot sin. That is the *absolute* truth. That is a judgment of faith as distinct from a judgment of experience. It arises from what we know of God, of Christ, not of human life. These texts of John's are all judgments of faith, formed from his knowledge of the absolute holiness and power of Christ. He has forgotten for the moment the actuality of man. He is possessed with the sense of the omnipotence of Christ. That will be *finally* as actual as it is now ideal. It is the ultimate reality. It is the surest thing in existence. John was speaking from the interior of Christ, possessed by the faith of His moral omnipotence. The words were not written by a man who had attained sinlessness, or watched it in others, and then worked out its implications backward to Christ. They came from one who by faith and not experience had grasped this nature, power, and place of Christ.

Experience works up from nature to infer God's power and glory; from human love to infer a divine tenderness and fatherhood; from personal history to implications about Christ and God. And that is the method of a subjective, literary, and humanist age like the present. But faith works downward from its grasp of God in Christ alone, from its absolute and eternal certainties, to actual life. And it works not merely with an inference but with an ought; not with implications but with compulsions; with demands absolute in order to be final and effective; not upon thought or truth, but on conduct. It does not induce from life what God must be, but it deduces from God what life must be. It does not predicate about God: it prophesies about man. The experimental religion of true faith is not based on experience, but on revelation and faith. It is *realised* by experience, it proceeds in experience; but it does not proceed *from* experience. Experience is its organ, but not its measure, not its principle. What we experience we possess, but faith is our relation not to what we possess but to what possesses us. Our faith is not in our experience, but in our Saviour. It is not in our experience of our Christianity, but in a Christ Who, while we are yet without experimental strength, both dies and lives for us. John concludes from Christ to man as the normal man in Christ should be, as Christ alone is. It is not a logical but a Christological judgment. To abide in Christ certainly would be to escape sin. It would not be to acquire sanctity as a recompense for faith, but it would be to perfect that life

of faith which is the only sanctity.
He who sins does so because he hath
not seen Christ or known Him, has
not seen into Him and understood
Him. He has perhaps been thinking
of his own sin, and arguing up from
that experience that he must be out
of Christ, instead of dwelling on the
Redeemer and working down with a
spirit-compulsion on his own sin.
He has not grasped Christ's spiritual
omnipotence in temptation, has not
gone in upon Christ, but merely
hung on Christ. To hang upon
Christ, and to do no more than hang,
is to be a drag on Christ and a strain
on man. To see and know Him is
to enter and live in Him, to walk,
run, mount, by the communion of
His life. The fall of many who once
were Christ's is because they took no
serious means with themselves to
prosecute their life in Him, but were

dragged in His wake till they got
tired of the strain. There are men
to-day who once tasted Christ, but
their serious will was not given to
their Christian life but to their affairs.
And so the world, having monopolised
their *will*, submerged their soul. And
to be dragged after Christ, submerged
in a medium so dense as the world,
means a friction and a strain so
severe that they took their fatal
relief by cutting the cord — and
drifting.

8. I wish to lay much stress on the
vital difference between the saint's
sin and the sinner's sin, as these
texts carry it home to us. It has a
vital bearing on the question of a
sinful and a sinless perfection, the
perfection which is faith, and the
perfection which has outgrown faith
and become only rarefied character
or conduct. Any perfection which

does that has become another than
Christian perfection, and in leaving
faith behind has fallen from faith.

The difference between the Christian and the world is not that the
world sins and the Christian does
not.   It suits the world to think that
it is; because ᵕ offers a handy whip
to scourge the Church's consistency
while resenting its demands.   But
such a distinction is no part of the
Church's claim.   Nor does it mark
off the Christian's worldly years from
his life in Christ.   A difference of
that kind is merely in quantity—all
the sin on the one side, none of it on
the other.   But the real difference
(I must say often) is not in quantity;
it is in quality.   It is not in the
number of sins, but in the attitude
toward sin and the things called sin.
It is in the man's sympathies, his
affinities; it is in his conscience, his

verdict on sin, his treatment of it—
whether the world's or his own. The
world sins and does not trouble; it
even delights in it. In sin it is not
out of its element; it may even be
in its element and most at home
there. The fear and hate of sin is
not in the least its temper. But with
the Christian man there is a new
spirit, a new taste, bias, conscience,
terror, and affection. His leading
attitude to sin is fear and hate. His
interest, his passion, is all for good
and God. He himself is different
from himself. He is renewed in the
spirit of his mind. He may indeed
lapse. The old instinct, the old
habit, breaks out, and surprises him
off his guard. The old vice fastens
on him in a season of weakness.
The old indifference may creep back.
Mere nervous exhaustion may make
him feel for a long time as if the

spirit had been taken from him. But these are either interludes, or they are upon the outskirts of his real nature. The loyalty of his person is still sound; his compass is still true, and his course in the main is right, whatever deviations the storms may cause, or however the calms may detain and irritate him. What is the thing most deep and assertive in him? I mean, what is most continuous in him? I do not ask what asserts itself *oftenest*, but what asserts itself most persistently on the whole, and in the end most powerfully and effectively. What is the real and only *continuity* of his life? Is it a sinful temper and bias, a sinful joy or indifference, broken only occasionally, and ever more rarely, by spasms of goodness, glimpses of holiness, freaks of mercy and truth? Or is it the sympathy and purpose of holiness, clouded at times by drifts of evil, and cleft, to his grief, by flashes of revolt? That is the question. And it is the way the question will be put at the last. It will not be, How many are your sins and how many your sacrifices? but, On which side have you stood and striven, under which King have you served or died? A man may abide in the many-mansioned, myriad-minded Christ, even if the robber sometimes break into his room, or if he go out and lose his way in a fog. You stay in a house, or in a town, which all the same you occasionally leave for good or for ill. The question is, What is your home to which your heart returns, either in repentance or in joy? Where is your heart? What is the bent of your will on the whole, the direction and service of your total life? It is not a question settled in a quantitative way by inquiry as to the occupation of every moment. God judges by totals, by unities not units, by wholes and souls, not sections. What is the dominant and advancing spirit of your life, the total allegiance of your person? Beethoven was not troubled when a performer struck a wrong note, but he was angry when he failed with the spirit and idea of the piece. So with the Great Judge and Artist of life. He is not a schoolmaster, but a critic; and a critic of the great sort, who works by sympathy, insight, large ranges, and results on the whole. Perfection is not sinlessness, but the loyalty of the soul by faith to Christ when all is said and done. The final judgment is not whether we have at every moment stood, but whether: having done all we stand—stand at the end, stand as a whole. Perfection

is wholeness. In our perfection there
is a permanent element of repentance. The final symphony of praise
has a deep bass of penitence. God
may forgive us, but we do not forgive
ourselves. It is always a Saviour, and
not merely an Ideal, that we confess.
Repentance belongs to our abiding in
Christ, and so to any true holiness.

We may be essentially parted from
our sin while yet it hangs about us.
The constitution is renewed, but the
disease recurs in abating force. The
new nature asserts itself over the
head of reactions. We lust for the
fleshpots of Egypt, and we return
upon our tracks and move in a circle;
but it is, after all, but a loop upon
our larger line of onward march. The
enemy is beaten, though he makes
guerilla raids and carries off something we deplore. Our progress is
a series of victories over receding

attacks which sometimes inflict loss. And the issue turns on the whole campaign, not on a few lost battles. We sin, but we are not of sin. We are its master, though at times the convict seizes the warder and gets him down. But it does not *reign* in us. It is not our life-principle, though it may get expression in our life. We sin, but not unto death. We still have and still use the Advocate with the Father. Against our sin we plant ourselves on God's side. There is that strange power in us to be two yet one, to be a seventh of Romans, to face ourselves, yea to face a divided self, as if we were three in one, and to say No with the total man to a sin which exhorts a partial or occasional Yes. Every act of faith is saying No to a sin which says Yes in us. And sometimes the Yes drowns the No, while on the whole the life in faith says Yes to God. We lose on items, but we gain on the whole account. We are free from sin before we are rid of it, and of *all* its effects we are never rid. To all eternity we are what our sin has made us, by God's grace to it either as taken or refused. At our eternal best we are what redemption has made us, and not sanctification alone. We enter heaven by a decisive change, and not merely by a progressive purification. And this is the very marrow of Protestant divinity and Evangelical faith.

9. I should not like to be thought to mean that if the regenerate sin, it is not really they who sin but the flesh in them, the old man still surviving but not affecting their will. If the will were not affected the struggle would not be so severe, nor the tragedy of the conflict so intense.

The passion and pity of Romans vii. would not be the classic and searching thing it is and always has been if it were only a will at war with a tendency. It is two wills at war. It is at least a divided will. 'It is no more I that do it, but sin that dwelleth in me' cannot mean that the will is wholly on the right side, but that in some slumber of it the dark unholy element wakes to seize the helm and give the course. That would be sad and mad, but not so bad as the awful situation whose despair calls for the redeeming intervention of the Son of God. The sin dwelling in the man is a sinful will, sinful volitions. It is not as if he *had* sin, but did not *do* sin. Sin is essentially an act of the will. And our acts cannot be severed from our central will in the way that these extenuations suppose. There is nothing in a man deeper than his source of action. There is no central something which can be the subject of sinlessness, a holy *Ding an sich*, while the casing of it is spotted with transgression which is not fatal because it is peripheral. Such psychology is mediæval, Catholic, and outgrown. There is nothing at the core which is unaffected by the act of sin. When sin is done, it is the man that sins. In each act which is not a mere occurrence it is the personality that is involved. Anything done in us, to us, or through us, is not an act, and is not sin, however damnable the sin is that may be the source of it outside us. There comes to my mind Shelley's *Cenci* and its preface.

In the sinful act it is the personality that is involved at its centre, but it need not be involved in a fatal and final way. It is very rarely that any single act embodies and exhausts the *entire* personality. That were the sin unto death, or else the divine act that as decisively redeems. And in either case the act is the compendium of a whole series of acts, which expresses the character of the personality. Acts may be done by the will, good or evil, which involve the personality from its centre, and ᴠ affect it, but do not seal and decide it for ever. The will may sin, but the personality, the *series* of volitions, the ruling habit and character of the will, is not given up to evil, and has not chosen it as its good. There may be sinful volitions in us, and yet the sinful principle does not really own us, but the good. 'It is no more I that do it' does not mean that it is not his will; for it is. But it does mean that it is not his total, ruling, and distinctive personality that does it. Sin captures certain volitions, but not the whole personality that exerts the volition. The sin comes from the centre, but it has not its home in the centre. Each sin comes from the central will, but not from the focus of the personality. It is a case of two sets of volitions, one of which is a chain, and the other a mere series. The evil volitions do not cohere in habit and affection. The man may put his whole force at any mad moment into a simple volition, but not his whole personality. *As* the new and regenerate personality he does not sin; and he cannot, in this sense, till the frequency of the sinful volitions, and their neglect, forge them into a chain, and bind the personality under them. It is not sin in the final sense till the sinful volitions are multiplied and spread through his personality, giving it its habit and affection, and dyeing it to the colour of evil. Passion becomes vice, and vice becomes his element.

10. The coherent and continuous line in our Christian life is the line of faith. The sins make a certain series, but broken, scattered, irregular. They emerge, but they do not make the continuity. They may bend the continuous line, or bury it, but they do not break it. They are foreign to us and not germane. What is germane is Christ and faith. Our prevailing habit of soul and bent of will is Christ's. And our falling out may even be (by His grace and our serious treatment of it) but the renewal of love. The fellowship is interrupted, but the base of the character is unchanged. The soul is not subverted. A cable still con-

nects the two shores—Christ's and ours. If it break at a place it can be mended by pains, and connection restored. But the habit of sin, the worldly mind, takes the cable away. While it is there, defect is not destruction. 'A sectary,' says the Apostle to Titus, 'after the first and second warning reject, knowing that he is subverted and sinneth, being judged by himself.' There was no subversion, no sin unto death, in his sinful acts, till, in the face of light and warning, they became inveterate, a second nature, the ruling, perverse, crusted habit of his life. It is not sins that damn, but the sin into which sins settle down. Good and evil co-exist in the believer as in the re-deemed world. But they co-exist in a very different way; the currents set differently; the proportions are different; and it makes all the difference whether they are at the centre or the circumference of the soul, whether they are in its citadel or its suburbs. There is sin as the principle of a soul and sin as an incident, sin which stays and sin which visits. Visitations of sin may cleave indefinitely to the new life, and the freedom to sin and the risk are always there. The great justification does not dispense with the daily forgiveness. There is the great forgiveness once for all, when the man passes from death to life, to a new relation with God; and there is the daily forgiveness which renews it in detail and keeps the channel of grace clean, once it has been cut, and prevents it from silting up. There is the great forgiveness from sin which we ask in Christ's name alone, and there is its detail in the daily forgiveness which depends also on our forgiving daily.

There is the bathing of the whole man into the regeneration in which he is born of God, and there is the washing, which is the cleansing of the feet daily exposed and daily soiled. There is all the difference between the pardoned sinner and the pardoned saint, between the step out of the world and the steps up to God. We have to work out into practice what we are in principle, to become what we are and are not, to fight sins because we are freed from sin. And failures in practice, however dangerous, are not the same as the great failure to place ourselves on the side of righteousness and holiness all our days.

It is easy to see the moral value of these great spiritual truths, the greatness, amplitude, magnanimity, freedom, they lend to life. It is always thus with the great spiritual realities. Apart from their direct and conscious power over us, they have an indirect power in us which we but partly know. We acquire their habit. We take life nobly. We escape from moral or mental scrupulism. We teach mere accuracy its true place, and we rescue veracity from the pedagogue for the seer, from Fröbel for Carlyle. We rise above the bondage of the small moralities and punctilios of life, to a noble carelessness which is the truest duty to details and the condition of doing them justice, and no more (which would be less). We walk in the spirit, and escape the importunities of the flesh. It is only so that we are fair to both flesh and spirit. To treat life as a whole is the only justice to the parts of life. And this wholeness of vision, this totality of soul, it is not given even to Art to create,

but to Jesus Christ. There have
been certainly more magnanimous
and patient Christians, in proportion,
than artists. To see life most steadily
and whole is, after all, the gift of
Christ, as it was the power of Christ.
He saw the soul from its centre and
from its height. And the bane and
travail of the world-soul was His,
and only His, in the most real and
effective sense. The true, sound, and
steady view of life does not belong
to man's criticism of life, even when
the phrase means poetry; it belongs
to the judgment of God, Who judges
the world in Christ. He judges best
who judges last. It is the final
judgment that is the soundest. And
that is the judgment of Christ, and
of those whose moral and spiritual
discrimination are cultivated with
Him. Thus we are at once saved
and judged. Salvation is quite as

much judgment as privilege. And being judged, we sit secure upon the world. There is no fear or favour to deflect our own judgment. We are united with Him Who is Himself the final, and therefore faultless, Judge. Know ye not that the saints shall judge the world? The final sanity is complete sanctity. And the Holiest is the Key to the whole.

II

SANCTITY AND FAITH

'Every man *perfect* in Christ Jesus.'
Col. i. 28.
'Complete in Him.'—Col. ii. 10.

CHRISTIANITY is the perfect religion because it is the religion of perfection. It holds up a perfect ideal, it calls us *incessantly* to this ideal, and it calls *all* to this ideal. *Each* man is called, and each man is *always* called, to it. It is a religion that issues from the perfect One, and returns to His perfection. But it returns through a far country and a dread. It returns by way of Redemption, so that the means of reaching this per-

fection for us sinners is not achievement but faith.

Christianity is not the perfect religion in the sense of being revealed
as a finished, rounded, symmetrical
whole. It is not perfect in the sense
of a closed circle, or a plastic form,
which can be altered in nothing
without being spoiled. It is not a
perfection of proportion, of harmony,
of symmetry. That is the Greek,
pagan idea of perfection; whereas in
Christianity we enter the perfect life
maimed. The pagan idea of perfection is balance, or harmony of parts
with each other. It is self-contained
and self-poised. The Christian idea
is faith, or harmony of relations with
the will and grace of God. It is self-
devoted, complete in Him; the perfection not of finish but of faith. It
is perfect, not because it presents us
with perfection, but because it puts

us in a perfect attitude to perfection.
Our perfection is not some integrity
which we *possess*, in the sense in
which the Vatican possesses the faultless Venus, or Christ's infallible Vicar.
The one is as pagan in its idea of
perfection as the other. It is the
æsthetic idea of mere consistency,
flawlessness, symmetry of thought
and order, external, palpable, and
unspiritual. But Christian perfection is something which we are put
in the perfect way to *realise*, in the
sense that we realise a living, moving
ideal of character and life. It is not
something with which we are presented; it is not even something we
are to *believe*; but it is something
into which we are *redeemed*. The
perfection of Christianity is not even
in the *ideal* of perfection it offers,
but in the *power* of perfection it
implants; not in its ideal of a Son of

God, but in the power it gives, with *the* Son of God, to become sons of God by believing in His name.

Moreover, the perfection of God in Christ is not only a universal demand, but an instant; it is something which we can and must enter on in this life. We cannot exhaust it in this or any life, but we can and must be among the perfect in this life. 'Be ye perfect' does not mean, Aim at a perfection in eternity, many lives and cycles away: the idea of cycles of development, however true, is foreign to the New Testament. It means, Enter here and now on the perfection of God.

There are two notions of perfection which are wrong, and a third which is right. But all three are right compared with the notion that we are to wait for perfection till some indefinite time in the infinite future. All three urge that Christian perfection is a condition of actual, living people in this world. It is a religion, a faith; it is not merely a hope.

The first idea is Pietist; the second is Popish; the third is Protestant, Apostolic, Christian.

1. The Pietist idea pursues perfection as mere quietist sinlessness with a tendency to ecstasy. Its advocates are people sometimes of great grace and beauty; but it represents a one-sided, narrow, and negative spirituality. Its religion is largely emotional, mystical, and introspective. Its adherents are apt to be the victims of visions and moods. They seek perfection in a state of sinlessness. It is a condition largely subjective, ascetic, anæmic, feminine. It prescribes an *arbitrary* withdrawal from the interests, pursuits, and passions of life. It is a cloistered virtue. It is *distrait*, not actual. There is

an absence of true humility. In its stead there may be either a laboured counterfeit, as painfully sincere as it is unsimple; or there is a precise self-righteousness which cannot veil a quiet air of superiority. It is certain that the perfect man will be the last to know how perfect he is. It is not a thing that can be worked at. For essential to all perfection is humility, and it is too humble to know how humble it is. In its choicer forms this pietism is devoted to love and prayer; but it seldom escapes the tinge of self-consciousness in their culture. In too many cases the prayer is superficial, mindless, without searching insight or passionate worship; while its love is limited, placid, and pale. Its holiness is to the great and classic sainthood, whether Roman or Protestant, as the drawing-room song is to music.

Moreover, this perfectionism is too individualist to feel how the single soul is tainted with the sin of its kind, and its possible achievement lamed by the slow progress of the race. The kind of perfection it aims at is made impossible by the ties that bind us to the part of mankind which is still unregenerate. And with all its introspection, it is too unpsychological to realise how the traces of sin live on in the sin-tainted will. Its self-examination is too mindless, too little mordant, for the individual, as it is too individual for the race. It knows of the exceeding sinfulness of sin, but its moral imagination is too poor to *realise* it. And there are some advocates of this sinless perfection who are offensive not only to the world, but also to the best of the Church. Their dulness of moral perception, commonness of fibre, and poverty of ideal breed a self-satisfaction which is little removed from Pharisaism. And for public life they are of little worth. They may belong to the National Church, but for want of spiritual freedom they show little interest in the crucial issues of national Christianity. Their treatment of Scripture is accordingly childish. But they abound in devoted philanthropy. They have done much to quicken missionary zeal. And it is a service to insist on the idea of perfection as a present demand and an unworldly call. Their chief error is the identification of perfection with sinlessness. It is not the will of God that in this life we should be sinless, lest we should find a perfection apart from forgiveness.

2. The Popish idea of perfection has much in common with the Pietist. It is unworldly in the negative sense;

it flees from the world, it does not master it. It is embodied in the monk and the nun. In the Roman system the monk is the ideal man, the nun the ideal woman. These stand on the summit of moral and spiritual greatness. They are likest Christ. They obey Christ most perfectly. Well, you have the Gospels in your hands. You have what Rome has—the Bible and the Holy Ghost. Do you find it so? Was Christ the Divine Monk? Did He recommend the cloister. Were His chief commands poverty, celibacy, and obedience to ecclesiastical superiors? To Rome the last of these is the greatest. Never forget that perversion. Was it so with Christ, with Paul?

The whole Roman system rests on the double morality involved in this distinction. It is a religion by double entry. It teaches that only some are called to perfection, while for the majority the demands made are much more ordinary. Rome succeeds, like certain governments, by lowering the educational standard for the masses, by not being too hard on the natural man. But it canonises a starved and non-natural man, on whom it is very exacting. It compounds for its laxity with its adherents by its severity with its devotees. There are *precepts*, it says, which all must obey, and there are *counsels* which are only for those few destined to perfection. There are the commandments of the moral law for all, and there are the counsels distinctive of the Gospel, like loving your enemies, or voluntary poverty, which are not commanded, but only advised for those who are set on perfection. The Roman Church reckons twelve of these. There are thus two grades of morality, two classes of men, two moral standards set up inside Christianity and inside the race. All are not alike before God. And all are not called to perfection in Jesus Christ; only a minority, only an aristocracy of Christians are. It is not said that only a minority attain, you will note; nor that those who respond to Christ are the true aristocracy of life amid a common world; but that only a minority of believers are *called* or intended by God for perfection in Christ. And these are not active but contemplative people, monks and nuns. *They* are the ideal Christian men and women. Whereas perfection in Christ is the essential call and badge of all Christians, and must be defined in harmony with that principle.

If the history of the monastic orders do not effectively destroy for

us that idea of perfection, we must
plunge, with Luther, into the principle
and gospel of the New Testament
again. I am not saying that human
nature rises up against that kind of
manhood. That would not be fatal.
For there are choice forms of Christian manhood, such as 1 Corinthians
xiii., which are not very welcome to
mere human nature, and not in its
power. If I hear a mere lusty
athlete, a lazy libertine, or a keen
worldling laughing at monks and
nuns, my Christian sympathies for
the occasion go to the cloister. I
become for the hour a pervert to
Rome. Mere natural manhood is
not the criterion of such things.
The Cross is against human nature.
But what does rise up against that
kind of perfection is the spirit and
principle of the Gospel, the faith
and freedom that broke forth from

the Cross, first in St. Paul, and then in the Reformation, which is our great Christian legacy and trust. These Pietist and Papist ideas of perfection are Catholic more than Evangelical, and thus are destroyed by the vital, free, final, sufficient, and perfect principle of Christian *faith*.[1] The true perfection is the perfection which is of God in *faith*.   The perfect obedience is not the obedience which is *associated with* faith or flows from it, but the obedience of the soul which *is* faith, and which is the saving power and perfection for all.   To be perfect is to be in Christ Jesus by faith.   It is the right relation to God in Christ, not the complete achievement of Christian character.

[1] It is remarkable how Rome has been fed by a debased Evangelicalism.   The early life of Newman is but one case of many.

The Protestant idea of perfection is the possession of the righteousness of God. And the righteousness of God, in the New Testament idea, is something which is a gift of God to us, and no achievement of ours before Him. It is a justification of us, a righting of us, effected by Him, and on our side appropriated by the obedience not of conduct but of faith. On the human side, indeed, it *is* faith, which is held by God to be our righteousness, our true adjustment to the ultimate moral reality, which is Christ. In faith we are in the right and perfect relation to God. But God's justification of us is a perfect and complete thing. In faith, therefore, we possess the perfect will of God concerning us. We enter on a full salvation. We have as ours the fulness of Christ. The Roman theology knows only of a perfection, a righteousness, which is an acquisition, which is always growing and never there, which is not complete in the act of union by living faith, but must always be eked out by the sacraments and the obedience of the Church. There is, indeed, a true sense in which the perfection even of faith grows. It becomes actual in life and practice; but that adds nothing to the perfection which is ours in the incredible salvation which we take home by supernatural faith. Faith is implicit; what is explicit is experience. We but unfold a perfection which is in God's sight *there*, we do not accumulate a perfection which we are always striving to place there. The queen and mother of all the virtues is not our subjection and obedience to the Church. Implicit faith in anything institutional is usurped faith. The true faith is implicit in Christ, in Whom are hid all the treasures of wisdom and knowledge. Faith is in its nature obedience, but it is the will's obedience to Christ. This is the root and mother of virtue; this is the new life with the promise and potency in it of all the perfection which may become actual in us by any sanctification. Our sanctification only unfolds in actual life the ideal perfection in which we really stand by faith in Christ. And yet this ideal perfection, being of pure and free grace, is not the vision foreseen by God of our moral effort's final success. But it is the finished and foregone gift of God in Christ through our faith, and the thing which alone promises the final success of any moral efforts. In giving Christ He gave us all things—*i.e.* perfection. It is not our moral success that is

E

presented as perfection to God even in anticipation; it is God's present to us of perfection that makes moral success possible. And this is the whole issue in the Roman controversy which the public on its cycles, newspapers, and political campaigns vainly thinks it has outgrown. The public thinks, but its soul does not. And so it thinks to little forward purpose and to little ultimate success. And it does not discern the most grave dangers to its own security and peace; which serious thought spiritually discerns in subtle and inchoate stages that need generations to work out their evil doom.

I cannot stop to trace how these popish ideas came in to distort the Gospel, how they rose in part from the old Stoic paganism and its mortifications. It could be shown you how Plato and Aristotle had much more to do with them than St. Paul. Almost everything wrong in Romanism is a case of pagan malaria, which crept in on the pure gospel of the New Testament, and which it is so hard to get out of the Christian system. The sacerdotalism of Rome, for instance, is much more pagan than Jewish in its origin and nature. So is the connection of Church and State. But I do ask leave to point out the root error that underlies these perversions, and a good many more, at this hour. Because I am not waging a polemic against Romanists; but as preaching to Protestants exposed to the • like paganism to-day, I wish to point out how these wrong practices rise out of pagan errors which many Protestants share, and especially out of a supreme belief in the natural man and his morality as the Christain ideal. As soon as you part with the idea that our perfection is in our faith and not in our conduct, you have taken the train for Rome; and I urge you to get out at the first stop and go back to another platform.

The error at the root of all false ideas of perfection is this : it is rating our behaviour *before* God higher than our relation *to* God—putting conduct before faith, deeds before trust, work before worship. That is the root of all pharisaism, Romanism, paganism, and natural and worldly morality. It is the same tendency at bottom which puts the sacraments above simple faith, which neglects the worship of the sanctuary for work in a mission, or replaces the gospel by ethical culture. 'I do not care about a man's belief,' you say; 'show me what he does.' Do you mean that? Now, I care comparatively little about what you do, but I care infinitely about whom you believe in. I know if you believe in Christ your conduct will be seen to; but I have no guarantee that if you behave well you will believe in Christ. You may only admire Him as the greatest success in your own moral line, a master in your own art, the victor in a conflict, which after all you regard as the same for Him and for you. And all that is something different in kind from trusting Him as your Redeemer through victory in a conflict different in its purpose from yours or all men's. Our Redeemer is not simply a master in a region where we are all amateurs, as a great painter is the idol of his craft. But do you quite mean what you were saying? Do you mean that, if a man is good to the poor and kind to his family, honest in business, and

active in humane politics, it is no
matter what he thinks about Christ,
whether he has to do with Him at
all, or how he stands to the Cross?
Do examine these phrases which
make a flattering appeal to common
sense. I suspect every creed which
in the name of religion appeals to
common sense. Do you really mean
that a man's relation to God and to
Christ is of little moment so long as
he is self-denying, generous, public-
spirited? If you do, you are popish
and pagan in principle. And if a
majority were of your way of thinking, we should have the Roman
Church re-established in this country
in a few generations. We should
have the ethical soil for it. It is
because that way of thinking and
speaking is so common among Protestants, in the spirit of the age, that
Romish principles have got so far with

us as they have.   It is because Christianity becomes identified with behaviour, with man's treatment of man,
with humanism, philanthropy, humanity, with kindness and pity instead of *grace*. Humanity! Why, as
Ibsen says, God was not humane to
His own Son. We are not saved by
the love we exercise, but by the Love
we trust. The whole Protestant issue
lies in that; and it is surrendered by
none more than by the philanthropic
liberals in popular theology. Their
sympathies have taken the reins from
their principles. They have lost in
'heart' the power of tracing principles
into their spiritual logic. They have
never *approfondi leur sentiment*.
We have no phrase for that admirable
expression more elegant than that
they have never sounded their own
sentiments, or realised their practical
sequel on a long historic scale. If

the perfection of a Christian man is in the morals or the mercy he exhibits and not in the Grace he trusts, if it is doing first and believing second, then the Romish form of Christianity is the sole and inevitable. It does not matter whether the doing is moral or ceremonial, behaviour or ritual.

The apotheosis of conduct has become a popular cult through the teaching of Matthew Arnold, so congenial to the British philistine and the semi-Roman Englishman. It is surely more accurate to call British philistinism Arnold's ally rather than his enemy when we remember that the Philistine was not the enemy of an Israel of ideas, as he said, but of an Israel of faith. It is Arnold's despised Nonconformity that represents the prophetic element in religion, which was the soul of the chosen people and the butt of Philistine mockery. And one may call the average Englishman semi-Roman, not only because in temperament he is the Roman of the modern world, but because, ecclesiastically, his moral culture and type have been so largely moulded by the half-reformed Church which he still tolerates, and which he prizes more as an organisation of energy and society than of faith. It is a premiated institution of law and works. Well, for Arnold religion was a branch of culture. It was ethical culture, aided by the spiritual imagination. And the Church was to be supported, even by the agnostic, as the great society for the promotion of goodness or conduct, which he memorably defined as 'three-fourths of life.' Like most worship of culture and of the orderly æsthetic idea of perfection, Arnold's work makes ultimately for Rome. Rome is the refuge

from his intellectual doubt.   Rome is
the home of his imaginative religion.
Rome realises his idolatry of good
form.   And Rome is the soil congenial
to his ethical nomism, his moral
ritual, his religion of morality tinged
with emotion, of flushed conduct and
blanched belief.   All agnostic culture
leads to clericalism by lay indifference,
and then to Rome by desperation.   It
does not lead to atheism, because the
feminine side of human nature will
not endure that; it prefers large and
definite error to narrow vague truth,
positive peril to negative ruin.

But Christian perfection is not a
perfection of culture.   It is not a
thing of ideas or of finish.   Such perfection is for the select few, for a
natural elect.   It is the perfection of
the *élite*.   This is so even with ethical
culture.   Its fine programme is yet
no gospel.   The soul's true and uni-

versal perfection is of faith. It is a'
perfection of attitude rather than of,
achievement, of relation more than of,
realisation, of trust more than of behaviour. Conduct may occupy three-'
fourths of our time, but it is not
three-fourths of life. To say that it
is, is to return from the qualitative to
the quantitative way of thinking, from
which culture was expected to deliver
us. The greatest element in life is
not what occupies most of its time,
else sleep would stand high in the
scale. Nor is it even what engrosses
most of its thought, else money would
be very high. It is what exerts in-
trinsically the most power over life.
The two or three hours of worship
and preaching weekly has perhaps
been the greatest single influence on
English life. Half an hour of prayer,
morning or evening, every day, may
be a greater element in shaping our

course than all our conduct and all
our thought; for it guides them both.
And a touch or a blow which falls on
the heart in a moment may affect
the whole of life in a way that no
amount of business or of design can
do. Conduct is not the main thing.
To say that it is, is but the pardon-
able extravagance which gives force
to a necessary protest. Look to the
faith and the conduct must come.
True faith has all ideal conduct in its
heart and, what is more, in its power.
And it is the only thing that has it.
Yea, the main thing is not conduct;
and it is not even character. Action
may shape character. But what shapes
action? And it is not action alone
that shapes character. It is something more akin to faith that shapes
both. There are forms of Christianity
which preach character—character,
as if that were the saving thing, the

thing to work at, as if it were healthy
to work at it. It is no more the
saving thing than conduct. It is not
the soul's perfect state. It is a thing
of greatest moment, but it is the fruit
of salvation, the expression of our
perfection, not its condition. It is
the result of being accepted by God;
it is not what makes us acceptable.
A person of no character may by
faith be more acceptable to God than
one whose soulless character is in
universal esteem. Else what is the
meaning of the penitent thief, of
publicans and harlots going into the
kingdom of heaven before decent
Pharisees? Do you think that Pharisees there meant only the rascals of
the party, the quacks, the impostors,
the conscious hypocrites and pious
frauds? Did it need the moral insight and the spiritual authority of
Jesus to tell us that a penitent out-

cast was preferred before these? No. Anybody could see that. He meant that the reprobate, in his act of faith, with his character not only lost but ruined and all to be built up again— that that reprobate was, in the passion of his penitence and trust, inside the kingdom of heaven; while the reputable Pharisee, the esteemed and estimable member of the national party and the national church, whose uprightness and respectability had been such as never to rouse the need of repentance, was without. Yea, the hard, placid matron whose family was well brought up and floated out, who was a patron of society, a sponsor for all new-comers, a chaperone with whom you could go anywhere, she was outside the Kingdom; and poor Magdalene, poor Gretchen, the poor slayer of her unwelcome child, might be in. If that was not Christ's view,

what does the story of the prodigal
and his brother mean? The prodigal
had no character at all; and his
brother's character was fit to be held
up to all the young farmers of the
country-side. But the prodigal had
faith and repentance. And in these
he had a perfection before God denied
to ninety-and-nine too admirable to
need repentance. It is not a question
of the sinless being postponed to the
sinful and repentant. It is not a
case of premium on sin and evil-
doing that good may come. It is a
case of a sinful race, whose one true
attitude to God is penitence, and
which is more worthily represented
in God's sight by the repentant
prodigal than by the lives (so charm-
ing to our social and friendly associa-
tions) to which personal sin seems as
strange as the sting of it is unknown.
I am not impugning social position,

or our personal affinities, affections, and admirations. Society has its rules, which must be recognised; and our natural love and esteem have their own place. They are wholesome on the whole. They are based on merit, on character; and they should be. They must rest on something of which men and women can take cognisance. It is men and women that are the judges. The vice of Pharisaism (as it was Israel's ruin) is that it makes the divine standard the same in its nature; it puts merit everywhere and grace nowhere; it makes the divine ideal to be a matter of our achievement, the divine favour a reward for our goodness; it makes the divine welcome to turn on what we have done, or on what we have grown to be, instead of on faith in the grace which delights to make new men out of our worthless-

ness and our impotence to grow at
all. The saints, in the New Testament, are not the saintly but the
believing. What Christ always de-
manded of those who came to Him
was not character, not achievement,
but faith, trust. His standard was
not *conduct*, it was not *character*, it
was not *creed.* It was faith in Himself as God's Grace. It was trust,
and trust not in His manner but in
His message, His gospel. That was
the one demand of God; and to
answer it is perfection. Obedience
to God's one comprehensive demand
must be perfection. 'This is His
commandment, that ye should believe in Jesus Christ.' That is to
say, *perfection is not sanctity but
faith.* It is the obedience which *is*
faith. Do not miss the real point.
Perfection is obedience. Good. Rome
says that. It is the obedience of faith.

Rome says that too. She says it is that obedience to the Church which grows out of belief in the Church. No! The obedience of faith is not the obedience which grows out of faith, but the obedience which faith is, which constitutes the act of faith, in which it consists. It is that surrender of the *will* which is involved in the act of personal faith in the living, saving Person of Jesus Christ. That is Christian perfection. All other excellence flows from that. All ideal perfection is latent in that. All moral character, all sanctity, is in its germ in that. The man of faith is perfect before God because his will and person is in the relation to God which is God's will for him. And he has the germ and the conditions which will work out in sanctifying time to ethical perfection as well. But that holy perfection, that perfection of character, is there already to the eye of God, Who sees the end in the beginning, and the saint in the penitent.

Let no mistake linger, then, in your minds. Christian perfection is the perfection not of conduct, character, or creed, but of faith. It is not a matter of our behaviour before God the Judge, but of our relation to God the Saviour. Whatever lays the first stress on behaviour or achievement; on orthodoxy, theological, moral, or social; on conformity to a system, a church, a moral type, or a code of conduct; on mere sinlessness, blamelessness, propriety, piety, or sanctity of an unearthly type, — that is a departure from the Gospel idea of perfection; which is completeness of trust, and the definite self-assignment of faith amid much imperfection. To put these things, which are of second

and third rank, into the first place, as
we have been doing, is to get the soil
ready for all the crop that Rome can
so skilfully rear. It is the Catholic
debris left in Protestantism. It is a
nomistic, synergistic survival from
mediæval theology. It is the Protestant contribution to the Catholic
reaction of the day. Once grant
Rome's premises, and her use of them
is masterly. Once place religious
perfection outside of personal faith
in God's grace in Christ, and Rome
is master of the situation and of the
world. In a word, Christian perfection is the faith which justifies, puts
you right with God ; it is not culture
and sanctification by effort. Sanctification is not a perfection added to
justification. It is the spirit of it
drawn out, that perfection which is
all there latent (and to God's eye
patent) in justifying faith. The faith

that seizes Christ and makes Him its own already holds perfection.

Faith! Hold, understand, define it well. It is the condition of the Church's salvation and the State's. Do not waste your antagonism upon inferior dangers and false opposites. Some of us, perhaps, are easily excited about ritual. We dread its incoming as the stealing in of Rome. That grand old warfare of our fathers (who really understood the case), in the name of faith against *works*, has dwindled into a squabble among us about Protestantism and *ritual*, as if ritualism were the greater peril to Protestantism. That is being led by the eye, not by the mind and not by the soul, by sight and not by insight. All worship, however Protestant, must have some ritual. It is ritual to stand to sing, and bend, or kneel, to pray. It is ritual to

have a fixed order of service. The
question of a little more ritual or a
little less is a small one. A greater
question is what is *meant* by the
ritual, be it less or more. Is it the
ritual of a minister or of a priest?
That is the point. It is not, ritual
or no ritual. To have a minister at
all is to have a ritual. The real
question is as to the place of ritual,
small or great, in salvation. Does
salvation depend on the acts done
either by the congregation or in its
name—upon sacraments? And the
subtlest question of all is about a
kind of ritual which seldom strikes
the anti-ritualists as the great peril
—I mean the ethical ritual of life,
conduct, human acts, and achieve-
ments of any kind, however good,
offered to God as our hope of salvation and ground of welcome. Paul,
Luther, the Puritans, saw this real,

large, subtle meaning of ritual. The
ritual question was to them a mere
phase of the great battle of grace
and merit, faith and works. When
Paul condemned salvation by works,
perfection by the law, was he only
thinking of the ceremonial law? No.
It was all one law for him. The law
was a unity, including the Decalogue
as well as the priestly code. He
found no more salvation in the Ten
Commandments than in circum-
cision. His protest was against salvation by conduct, salvation by doing
things, perfection by character, welcome by merit, by anything except
absolute trust in the work of Christ
as the grace of God. Our chief
danger to-day is not the ceremonial
ritual, but the moral and social
ritual. It is the idea that men are
to be saved by well-doing, by integrity, by purity, by generosity, by

philanthropy, by doing as Christ did
rather than trusting what Christ did,
by loving instead of trusting love.
We object to the mass because
Christ's sacrifice cannot be repeated.
But self-sacrifice, which *only imitates*
Christ instead of sacrificing the self
to Christ, which would die *with* Him
before it has died *to* Him, is the
same spirit as Rome lives on. It
asks what Christ would do rather
than what He is doing. It is doing
as Christ did without appropriating
what He did. It is ethical ritualism
rather than spiritual service, copying the Lord's death Who has gone
rather than showing it forth till He
come. That is the frame of mind
which is *in spirit* so akin to Rome,
even while its antagonism may be
bitter against Rome; whose presence
in the air develops all the Roman
germs in our semi - Reformation.

Wherever you find the idea that the *first* condition or the *true* response to God's grace is *doing something*, there you have the habit of mind from which Rome has everything to gain and Christianity at last everything to lose. The 'Christian Agnosticism' which we are assured is the religious tone of the Universities offers more to Rome than to faith. And the way in which the public mind has become misled and trivialised in this question may be seen thus. You will find that some who are most ready to say, 'A fig for belief! give me character and conduct,' are the very people who are most suspicious about ritual in church, even when it only contributes to the decencies of worship. It is the old story of boggling at a midge and swallowing a camel. And what is the hope of Protestantism when the spiritual sense is so perverted, so externalised, so lost to the real and relative value of things? Such ethical ritualism is really more dangerous to the Protestant principle of Faith than much ceremonial.

Most ministers will know that what I say is true. And many laymen may complain that they do not know what I mean. So much has the rejection of theology destroyed the sense of the real situation in the *haute politique* of the Spirit, and the great issues of the Kingdom.

Your faith (that is, your soul) may be perfected when everything else is very crude and fragmentary. Your attainments even in grace may be very poor, but your faith may be perfect. You may utterly trust Him Who saves to the uttermost. You may perfectly trust your perfect Lord, and charge Him with the responsibility both for your sin and your sanctification. The perfectness of their trust is the only perfect thing about some; but it gives them perfection which people envy who are far richer in attainment and repute. Perfect faith is possible to some who, with many excellences, have no other perfection whatever. There are imperfect human beings whom we perfectly trust and love. There are faulty wives and husbands, parents and children, lovers and friends, who perfectly trust and love each other. There is no faculty so universal as this of perfect trust. How common it is I do not say; but it is the most universal in its nature. It is possible to those who can do nothing else. The child can exercise it. You can win it from many who are the despair of every other means of culture. The savage can learn it towards his missionary, and still more towards Christ, when he is too low in the scale to acquire much from civilisation beyond its vices. The perfection of faith is the hope of a universal religion. It is the great faculty of manhood. It is the great beauty of manhood and womanhood. It is the divine thing in love. It is the soul of marriage, whether of man and woman, or of mankind to Christ. Faith is the marriage of God's perfection and man's. It is the union of the perfection which is absolute and eternal with the perfection which is relative and perfectly *grows*. It is the human ideal, the supreme exercise of human faculty. It is an incessant demand on us, and it is an opportunity not for an elect but for all, not for a caste but for the soul.

P.S.—I regret that space does not allow me to enlarge the point, so grave and subtle now, which I have touched in the note on page 62. As I have dwelt on the effects of religious ethicism, so I should like to have drawn explicit attention to the Catholicising effect of a pietism which *practically* makes sanctity the first thing and faith only second, and would think more of Faber than, say, Livingstone. This quietism is a *pax Romana* in its inner nature and long result. There is a thirst for 'consecration' which is not the true way to holiness ; and a worship of saintliness which impairs the great sanctity.

III

GROWTH AND PERFECTION

'Not as though I were already *perfected*.'
PHIL. iii. 12.
'Let us who are *perfect* be thus minded.'
PHIL. iii. 15.

A DISTINGUISHED Frenchman has said that the idea of perfection is more to men than examples of it, and that this is equally so in art and morals.

In religion, it might be added, what we need more than either the idea or the example is the guarantee of perfection.

In morals, in character, the aphorism is certainly true. The love of perfection is more precious than the sight of it. An *example* of perfection often ties us down to a literal imitation of his manner of life, instead of kindling us to a fellowship of his spirit. This has happened with Christ Himself. He has been so treated as our perfect Example that His outward fashion of life has been copied at the cost of His inward principle. His poverty, celibacy, and freedom from civic duties—such things have been copied as if they were divine ends for every man, instead of means for a particular man's particular work. And the monks, thinking more of imitating Christ than of trusting Christ, lost the way of life in Christ's mere way of living. They lost the mind of Christ, and the true sense of Christ's unique saving work, till the Reformers set things mightily right. The *idea* of perfection, on the contrary, is a constant call to escape, through all the ascending forms in

which perfection has been expressed,
into sympathy with the principle that
struggled in them to light. Every
finite perfection is outgrown as the
infinite is more fully revealed. The
very Christ after the flesh becomes
inadequate to the Christ according
to the Spirit. He had to be broken
and die for His full scope. He
entered maimed into His eternal life.
The earthly life of Christ was perfect
in this sense, that it was perfectly
ruled and ordered by His task, it was
perfectly adapted at each stage to
carry out *His* purpose in the world,
and to finish the work given Him to
do. The same manner of life would
not be perfect, or even useful, for you
or me, to whom His work of Redemption is not given. But there is a
sense in which Christ lives more perfectly in His Church to-day than He
did in the form of His thirty years

on earth.   He is more universal, more
free from limitations of time and
space, more invisible in His action,
less exposed to the risks of Messianic
misconception.   We are less tempted
to do exactly as He did, and we are
better taught to trust what He did,
and then let our faith take a free,
spontaneous, and individual form in
our social life to His praise.   What a
thinker in art or morals may call the
idea of perfection, that *we* call the
Spirit of faith and fellowship.   And
our faith and fellowship in Christ is
worth far more for our perfection
than any effort to live up to Him as
our example—useful as that may be.
We are complete in Him, not merely
by His help but by His indwelling.
We are organised into Him.   It is
better, of course, to imitate the example of Christ than to be conformed
to the world.   But it is better to

trust Christ and His work than even to imitate Him. He is worth infinitely more to the world as its Saviour than as its model, as God's promise than as man's ideal. He is more to be admired than copied, more to be loved than to be admired, and He is to be trusted more than all. This trust of Christ is the highest thing a man can do. Trust become habitual is our new nature, our perfection made perfect, our life and abiding in Him.

When Christ bids us be perfect as our Father in heaven is perfect, He does not tell us to do what the Father does. The Father makes His sun to rise on the evil and the good, and sends rain on just and unjust. We cannot do that. We cannot affect sun or rain. We cannot copy God. He is Almighty as we are not. He is, to our great blessing, unseen. To

our great blessing Christ is now
unseen also. If we could see them
we might be copying them, or trying
and failing. What they do we know
not now. Their method of procedure
in the world we cannot trace, else we
might ruin their plans by poor imita-
tions of them which would be no
more than parodies, like Sheldon's
tales. We are not told to do *what*
God does, but *as* He does. It is
sympathy that is wanted more than
imitation. What we are to imitate
is the love and grace of God. And
there is only one way of imitating
that, only one way of learning it. It
is by trusting Him. Love is learned
by faith in the case of the unseen.
With our visible lovers faith may
come by love. With the Lover of
our souls love comes by faith. Love
of the unseen is the girdle of perfectness which is put on over the other

garments of faith and hope and all the virtues, and after them, as the last touch which keeps them all in form and place. The art of loving God is that perfection of educated *character*, that actual righteousness which is the result of long *sanctification*. But faith is that perfection of soul attitude to God, of rightness in relation to Him, which is our *justification*, our ideal righteousness, what used to be called an imputed righteousness. There is a perfection of character, you see, which is by sanctification. And there is a perfection of faith before the character has grown up under it, and that is justification. This is the perfection that makes the Church. The saints in the New Testament are not the fully sanctified, but the believers. The Church to-day is not a company of the sanctified, but of the justified.

They have only entered on their Christian manhood, they have not fully developed it. They are but spiritual adults, not spiritual heroes. And in the main, when the New Testament speaks of the perfect, it means not the complete but the spiritually adult; not the fully sanctified but the duly justified. They are not people who perfectly love, but who truly trust. They may be defective as yet in many points of character, or relations to each other. But they have entered on the right relation to Christ. They are not all ideal characters. Some are not even beautiful. But they will become so in time or eternity. They have started on that career. They have come to spiritual adultness by faith in Christ, as I say. They have entered on their spiritual vocation. But they have not yet reached spiritual distinction, when faith has its perfect work in love. Faith, therefore, in a sense is more than character because it makes character; and it is perfect before it makes character. But it is less than character; in the sense that the character may be only latent in it and not yet made.

The perfect, then, are those who by faith have settled into their divine place in the perfect Christ and become spiritually of age. You know the difference between a youth and an adult. There is a step taken in life, a step hard to describe and various in its ways, by which the boy passes into the man, the girl into the woman. They are held fit for a share in things to which they were not admitted before. They become initiates in life where before they had been novices. They cease, as it were, to be catechumens of Humanity and

become members. They graduate.
They are held fit to begin their real
education. They are admitted to
new circles, to new responsibilities,
new rights even in law. Things are
discussed with them which are not
discussed with boys and girls. They
acquire more or less common sense.
They become capable of learning
from life, instead of fluttering about
in it, or drifting. They stand on a
new footing, they are ready for
burdens, they are expected to cease
being carried and to begin to carry.
The soul, as it were, comes to itself,
settles into being itself. Its organism
becomes complete even if faculty is
not. The natural character reveals
itself in a distinct way. I do not
mean that all this takes place just
when people become legally of age—
at eighteen or twenty-one. With
some it may be about then, with

some later. I only mean that there
is a time when the natural character
passes out of the condition of crudity,
and rawness, and comparative imperfection, and enters a stage of
firmness, setness, and comparative
perfection. It is true of the body,
of the stature, and it is true of the
character and the will. They become
knit, compact, individual, character-
istic. That is becoming adult. It is
a step which is never repeated in life.
And yet it is not a final step by any
means. It is a perfecting of the
organism — the bodily organism or
the psychical, the moral, organism,—
but it is not the perfecting of the
character. It is the end of an age,
but it is also the beginning of an age.
Perfecting though it be, it is more of
a start than a close—like marriage,
which only in comedies ends all, but
in reality begins all, the serious part

of life. We become not so much perfect in the ordinary sense as *habiles*, capable, possible. When St. Paul says, 'We speak wisdom among the perfect,' he meant that he was talking as he would to spiritual *men* and not to hobbledehoys. He cast himself on their spiritual adultness, common sense, wisdom. It is as when Christ said, 'I speak as unto wise men; judge ye what I say.' What Paul meant was that, as he was not addressing the celestial and sanctified intelligences, so neither was he providing milk for babes, but speaking as a man to men in Christ Jesus.

Now it is a corresponding thing that takes place in the soul by faith. It is well to get rid of the idea that faith is a matter of spiritual *heroism*, only for a few select spirits. There are heroes of faith, but faith is not only for heroes. It is a matter of spiritual manhood. It is a matter of maturity. I have not used the word maturity, because it is ambiguous. It might be taken to mean the final fulness of power as well as the initial adequacy of power. Faith is the condition of spiritual maturity in the sense of adultness, of entering on the real heritage of the soul. It is the soul coming to itself, coming of age, feeling its feet, entering on its native powers. Faith is perfection in this sense. It is not ceasing to grow, but entering on the real and normal region of growth. It is starting on a progress through the scale of perfections. It is going on from strength to strength. Growth is then progress, not *to* Christ but *in* Christ.

I have not said that in *every* case in the New Testament this adultness, this coming of age, is the meaning of the word perfection. There are cases where it does have reference to some comparatively final stage of sanctification which is the goal of infinite hope in Jesus Christ. It means, sometimes, the state in which faith has worked out into love of God and man, into spiritual blessing and beauty, the abiding in Christ. Spiritual adultness and sanctification are not two perfections, but two aspects of the same perfection, which is the faithful soul's progress in faith to love. There is a bold passage in St. Paul (Phil. iii. 12), which makes this very clear. The two aspects of perfection meet in a point. He says he is not yet perfect, but in the next breath (v. 15) he says he is perfect: 'as many of you as are perfect be like me.' That is saved from being vanity by the fact that perfection is as conscious of what it is not as of

what it is. If you are in the right
and perfect relation to Christ, go on
to be perfected in Christ. If you are
in the way of Christ, let Christ have
His way with you. It is your perfection to be in a position in which
you are always being perfected. You
are perfect when you feel that Christ
has everything to do to perfect you.
To *believe* in Christ, to *be* in Christ,
and to *abide* in Christ, are three
stages of the same perfection—which
you may call the Petrine, the Pauline,
and the Johannine stages if you will.
A man is perfect when he comes to
belong to Christ instead of himself.
But he has for his goal, as Christ's
property, a perfection in which perfection itself is perfected. A man as
a Christian has entered on perfect
manhood, but he must always become
more and more so. Boys have
amused themselves with the puzzle

—how can the adjective perfect be compared? If a thing is perfect, can it be more perfect, or most? Well, if we were all circles, I suppose there would be no improvement possible. We should be complete—and empty. A perfect circle is done with. There could be no comparative degree. We should all be then what some believe themselves to be now—incomparable. But dead and done with. Unless, indeed, some ambitious circle had its life poisoned by the passion to rotate on its diameter and become a sphere. But if we were all perfect spheres we should be capable, I suppose, of no more perfection. We should be finished futilities. But as living souls our great perfection is the power of continually becoming what we are, coming to our true selves. As Christian souls, our perfection is in coming to ourselves in Christ.

We are perfect in Christ, and in Him continually more so. In Christ we are what we are to be—not in the sense in which a closed figure is all it can be, but in the sense in which the perfect seed has the promise and power of the perfect tree. Eternity is packed in our small souls. It is set in our heart. We are what we have to become. That is what gives faith its power and peace. In faith we are not panting, and straining, and rending ourselves after a perfection only ideal, possible, remote, and ever receding. We are not toiling to put achievement on the head of achievement, or mortification on the back of mortification, to reach heaven. That is a war of godless giants, which ends in failure, defeat, and chagrin. But we are unfolding a perfection which we already have in fee. We are appropriating what is already ours. We are sure that it is ours before it is on us. It is in us before it is on us. We have it with Christ before we have it with men. We are complete in Him before He completes Himself in us. We are perfect, and yet we are not perfect. We are as having nothing and yet possessing all things. We are in Christ, therefore we are complete; but we are in the world too, therefore we are not complete, but only on the way to completion. Our perfection, therefore, is not to be flawless, but to be in tune with our redeemed destiny in Christ. We are perfect, if not sinless. We are in Christ, even if we do not *yet* abide in Him. We are in the only relation which is capable of being perfected— the relation of faith. Faith as perfection is conformity to our high calling, which is also an upward calling. It is a perfection which both is and *grows*. True perfection is the power of perfect growth. But that does not mean unbroken growth. There are times when we lie becalmed, times when we have to tack, times when the current carries us astern, times when we are buffeted out of the straight course—when it is much if only we can keep at sea and not go to pieces on the rocks. Ignorance misleads us. Our charts fail us. Our crew mutinies, our passions take command, for a time. But, on the whole, we are on the living way. The master passion and bias of the soul is to Christ. The ruling will is the will of God, however certain impulses escape its control. We may still sin, but we are not sinners. Sin clings, soils, and may sometimes master. There are lapses, repentances, renewed forgivenesses. True perfection is not the power of unbroken growth, but of growing unto perfection, growing on the whole. The judgment is passed on our life-work as a whole. God does not judge us in pieces. He sees our life steadily, and sees it whole. The ship may be battered, but it comes to port, even though scarcely saved.

This note of growth is the most remarkable thing about Christian perfection. It has to sound so paradoxical, in order to be true. But, it is asked, does the perfect God grow? We are bidden to be perfect as He is perfect; is His perfection a thing of growth? No, indeed. The absolute God has all perfection in Him in actual completeness from first to last. We do not read that we are bidden to aim ⸜ at any of the absolute qualities of

God. That would be the old temptation, 'Ye shall be as gods.' How near
the devilish suggestion lies to the
divine, temptation to inspiration,
'Be as gods' to 'Be ye perfect'!
Our perfection is not to be rival
absolutes, but to love and trust the
absolute. Be as perfect in your
relative way as God is in His absolute
way, which contains all relatives.
Be as perfect men as He is perfect God. Meet God's will about
you in Christ as fully as God meets
his own view about Himself in
Christ. And the union of will and
nature in God is by love. It is not,
Be perfect fathers, but, Be sons
worthy of a perfect Father. But is
it such a strange and foolish thing,
this perfection which is and is not,
but only is to be? It is a mystery
but must it be a folly? It is noble
to strive. But would it be so noble

if there were not a perfection *in* our striving as well as *by* it, if we were not perfect while striving as well as while attaining? Is a perfect quest not part of our perfect good? If there were only perfection in attaining by striving, would not striving, effort, be outside the perfect life, or all perfection removed to another life? Is our striving not a part of our perfection? Is our perfection not, by the very nature and sanctity of effort, a growing thing?

Take an illustration also from your own personality. Go back ten, twenty years. Were you the same person as you are to-day? Yes, and no. Yes. For it was you then, as it is you now. There is something continuous. There is an identity which nothing can destroy. We do not believe that even death can destroy it. But also, No. You are not the

same. A great deal has come and
gone, and you are changed. You
have grown better or worse, but
you have changed. Every day has
changed you, and made you not the
man you were; you are either more
worthy of your personality, or less.
There is a case, apart from the life of
faith, a case from mere natural life,
of the same mystery of at once being
and not being, of being the same
yet not the same. You are a perfect
personality in the sense that you
are distinct from all others, adult,
complete in yourself, continuous in
your history, and so far consistent
with yourself that you are the same
person now as long ago. Yet this
perfection to which personality has
come in you is quite compatible with
a constant change and growth. So
much so, indeed, that if you had
ceased to change and grow it could

only have been by the dissolution of your personality itself. You only *are* because of your power to *become* what you are, to *grow*. Incessant growth is a condition of perfect living personality.

Again, take goodness. If a man say, 'I am now good, my moral education is finished,' it means that he gives up effort, gives up pursuing goodness. And that means that he ceases to be good. He has lost in the boast of possessing it the very thing he had. He has it only by a deep sense that he has it not but must always pursue it, win it, enlarge it, let it grow. That is true in the region of natural morality. It is still more true in Christ. We are only perfect in Him as we are in a condition to grow in Him.

Take, again, happiness. If you arrive at a condition in which you settle down and say, 'I will fix this day for ever so,' your happiness is doomed. 'Stay thus for ever, for thou art so fair.' The soul that says that to any earthly state has stood still with all the spiritual world moving. And the meaning of that must soon be that he is out of harmony with the world, and so happiness is gone. Happiness is a power of the soul to find its joy amid the constant change of experience, and to grow in mastery of a growing world.

So with culture and its love of the perfect. If it do not feel with the living time and grow to it, all its acquisitions become mere lore, mere pedantry.

So with character. If you freeze at the perfection of twenty or thirty, your character ceases to live and becomes mere mechanism, mere habit, prejudice, set grey life, moral death, and apathetic end.

You may ascend with the illustration to the character of Christ Himself. In what did His perfection consist? Those three years that we know—were they no more than the dramatic display of a perfection which was all finished before they began? Were they only like a photograph enlarged and thrown on a screen for the world to see—enlarged from a completed perfection existing in small in the Saviour's own soul? Or were they the perfection of real growth, the perfection of the growing life? In doing what He did for us, was He not doing something real for Himself? Surely His manifestation had in it nothing mechanical, nothing stagey. He was perfect at every point. That is, at every stage He was in perfect tune with the will of God.

He was perfectly equal to His unique work and the call of the hour. But it was the perfection of an ever-deepening note. Neither omnipotence nor omniscience was among His perfections. They were only those that pertained to His redeeming work. At every point He was completely obedient, but it was an obedience never completed till the Cross. He was perfectly obedient from the first, but He learned obedience by the things He suffered. His problem grew deeper on His gaze, his task grew more solemn as He moved into the deadly antagonisms of His time and the upper reaches of spiritual wickedness. He saw on the paschal night a cross He did not see in the rapture of His baptism, and He accepted then a work which He did not at first realise in its full form and fear. He was not more perfect in

His obedience at the end than at the beginning; but it was a more perfect perfection that He obeyed. Always perfect by faith, He was always being perfected in holiness. Always in the right relation to God, His realisation of God's will and purpose with Him ever deepened, and it was ever fully met.

And take as a last illustration the Great Redemption itself which His obedience wrought. It was completed in His death. It was finished. Having died unto sin once, it was once for all. That death and conquest needs no repetition. The sacrifice of the mass is an impeachment of Christ's finished work. It needs no supplement. The whole work was in principle done, the everlasting victory was in spirit won. In the spiritual world the Cross is one long indubitable triumph of conclusive bliss; and it would be so were every mass priest paralysed at the altar. What Christ did was a thing for ever complete and sufficient. Redemption is the condition of the world in God's eternal sight, and with it the perfect God is well pleased. With the world in the Cross, with the travail of the Redeemer's soul, He is satisfied.

But in *your* sight, actually, historically, is it a redeemed world? To your *faith* it is; viewed from this house, from this day, from this worship, from this pulpit, it is. It is so really, but is it actually? To your *sight* is it a redeemed world? Where is the perfection of Christ's work in yesterday's newspaper, in to-morrow's business, in the actual condition to which your soul has attained to-day, in the degree of sanctification reached by those who bow with you in the faith of the Cross, and put all their faith there? Where is Redemption in current affairs, in the course of past history, in the record even of the Church itself? It is so hard to see, that if we look away from the Cross we may not perceive it at all. 'And is the thing we see Salvation?' So hard to see, that even if we look at the Cross with the historian's eye alone, and not with the insight of faith, we mostly miss it. So hard to see, that even the Cross, even to faith's eye, might be ambiguous were its divine meaning not verified by the Resurrection. Yea, so hard to see, that Cross and Resurrection together might be dumb for us as to eternal issues were faith not fed by the witness of the Holy Ghost, and the Kingdom not assured by the perpetual working of its immortal King. For all the eternal and spiritual completeness of our Redemption, it is at the same time an imperfect thing, to many powerful spirits a thing denied. It is in history still, and for long must be, incomplete. It is in our experience very incomplete. An infinite perfection of Redemption is ours, and yet our Redemption is so imperfect. The work is finished, yet how unfinished are we, its products! That seems a strange and impossible thing; and the logicians might make great mirth of it were they not more than logicians — spiritual thinkers. The work is finished, not simply in the sense of being ended, but in the sense of being completed. The work is finished, not simply in the sense that the great Workman closed His day, and did His best, but in the sense that the task was completed, the end achieved, and He brought in eternal Redemption. The work is finished; but what unfinished things are we,

in whom the work must take effect!
Yes, Redemption is finished and unfinished, complete in heaven, incomplete on earth. Incomplete on earth,
with eternal promise and power.
Imperfect but no fiasco. We are
complete in Him in whom His own
work is always complete. He grasps
us by the Eternity within us—and
by the sin—to pluck out the sin and
develop the eternity. Our one perfection is to be in Him. He will
perfect Himself in us in His
time. Our perfection is the growing
perfection of faith in His absolute
redeeming perfection. We have a
perfect Redemption, however imper-
fectly redeemed we are at any one
stage. In faith we are what we can
never feel ourselves perfectly to be.
We are by faith what we are not, but
are ever growing by grace to be.

IV

PRACTICAL RÉSUMÉ

'Perfect in every good work.'—HEB. xiii. 21.

I WOULD end by resuming the more practical and experimental features of perfection.

Christian perfection cannot be thought of as an external thing, a formal thing, a thing completed and closed.

And yet our perfection must be a limited one. It is not possible for any Christian at any one time to fulfil all possible duties and realise all possible excellences. Your perfection lies in what is possible to *you* with *your* character and position, in

what *you* are called to be and do, in
what lies on *your* conscience, in what
concerns the situation in which *you*
find yourself in life. Duty is duty
for A as for B. But A's duty is not
B's. A's ideal of happiness is not
B's. A's love is not B's. A's idiosyn-
crasy is not B's. A's call is not B's.
There are limitations for each soul;
and in those limitations lies his freedom, his perfection. An unlimited
perfection is not possible. Even God
is limited, though it is by Himself.
But were it possible it would be a
great burden on us. An unchartered
freedom would only tire us. Our
freedom is *our* freedom. It has the
stamp of *our* character. It has a
charter in our individuality, a specifi-
cation, definite features, inalienable
qualities, distinctive of each one of
us. In our worst misery we dread
parting with ourselves and ceasing to

be. Our freedom and our perfection is not to be as gods but to find our place in God. And that we find by faith in Jesus Christ and growth in Him. Individual perfection is not possible apart from the perfection of all, especially as that is antedated in Christ. And the perfection of all is that each should be a member of the other in the Kingdom of God in the faith, service, and communion of Jesus Christ. Perfection makes his soul a whole; but it is a whole which is only perfected in *the* whole, in the Kingdom of God, under its conditions, its limitations. The most free and universal of all perfections was that of Jesus Christ. And in what narrow limits that perfection moved and grew! How it was perfected in the most awful agony and pressure of limitation the world ever knew—the weight and bondage of the Cross! In

His death He was crushed under all the sorrow and sin of the world. Every master finds his opportunity and realises his mastery in his limitations. It was the Cross of Christ that gave Him the world, the future, eternity, perfection, for a prey.

The features of Christian perfection are these. First, *faith*, as I have said. But I wish to define more Christianly the *kind* of faith. By faith I do not mean only that utterly inward transaction in which the soul forgets the world and deals with God, committing itself to Him in a high, spiritual, mystic, rapturous act. It is not the fine frenzy of religious emotion, the glow of exalted adoration and surrender. That may be in it, but that is not necessarily of it; it is not its test. There is a better test of faith than rapture. It is confidence, patience, and humility. Faith is not best expressed in boisterous assertions of assurance, however honest at the time, but in those forms of life and character. St. Paul's life-faith was greater than any of the finest expressions of it in his writings— partly because he never felt carried so high but that he might become a castaway if he did not take care. 'He that endureth to the end shall be saved.' Tune down your heroics to that; it is really tuning them up. Faith does not make you an angel cleaving the blue sky remote from the world. It makes you a son with the Father. It is not wings it gives you, but hands and feet to grasp and to go. Look at the extremes it avoids. At one extreme you may have incessant worry and care; at the other you have a carelessness about all the world so long as you are shut in with your religious dreams. Or at one end you have indifference, weak, spiritless, or desperate; at the other you have Stoic indifference, strong and proud. Faith is none of these things. It is filial trust in God's love, redemption, and providence amidst the duties, affections, pleasures, enterprises, perils, fears, guilts, gains, losses of active life. I do not say it is simple trust. It is not so simple, in the sense of being easy. You know well enough it is not easy to rise up out of those cares, absorptions, perplexities, impotencies of yesterday's work to a simple faith to-day. The greatest simplicities are not easy. And the simplicity of faith embodies all the difficulty of Christ with the modern world. And faith is not a piece of self-control. Nor is it a particular experience of life, or insight into life like a genius's. It rests on an experience of Jesus Christ and God's grace in Him. It rests in God amid much ignorance; though we do not know the future, and do not understand the past. It saves us from being victims of the world. It gives us mastery over it. It is the soul of sonship. It consists more of obedience and quiet confidence than of visions. And at the last it approves itself better (as I say) in *humility* and *patience* than in ecstasies. It is more faith to cleave to God in the dark hour of life and the dull commonness of duty than to throw ties, duties, services away, and seek a religion principally of sweet seasons and uplifted states. It is better to trust God in humiliated repentance than to revel in the sense of sinlessness. It is better to bear the chastening of the Lord as sons than to feel in the angelic mood of those who know they need no repentance. It is better to come home weeping than to stay at home self-satisfied.

It is not very often, comparatively, that the New Testament writers offer Christ as our example. But when they do, it is almost always in connection with His humility and patience and self-sacrificing love. It is His spirit, His faith and love, that are our example, not His conduct, not His way of life.

Humility is a frame of perfect mind not possible except to faith. It is no more depression and poverty of spirit than it is loud self-depreciation. It rests on our deep sense of God's unspeakable gift, on a deep sense of our sin as mastered by God, on a deep sense of the Cross as the power which won that victory. It is not possible where the central value of the Cross is forgotten, where the

Cross is only the glorification of self-sacrifice instead of the atonement for sin. A faith that lives outside the atonement must lose humility, as so much Christian faith in a day like this has lost it, as so much worship has lost awe. It is very hard, unless we are really and inly broken with Christ on the Cross, to keep from making our self the centre and measure of all the world. This happens even in our well-doing. We may escape from selfishness, but it is hard to escape from a subtle egotism which it is not quite fair to call selfish. This personal masterfulness of ours needs mastering. In many respects it is very useful, but it must go ere God in Christ is done with us. And it is mastered only by the Cross as the one atonement for sin.

Humility is a great mystery to itself. It is the amazement of the redeemed soul before itself, or rather before Christ in itself. It may take the shape of modesty before men, or it may not; humility is not anything which we have in the sight or thought of other men at all. It is the soul's attitude before God. 'Hast thou that faith? Have it unto thyself' before God. It can take very active, assertive, and even fiery shape in dealing with men. It is not timidity or nervousness. It is not shy, not embarrassed, not hesitant, not self-conscious, not ill at ease, not a seeker of back seats or a mien of low shoulders and drooping head. Yet it is not self-sufficient in a proud and Stoic reserve, nor self-assertive in a public Pharisee fashion. It can never be had either by imitating the humble or by mortifying the flesh. Devotion is not humility, though humility is devout. It is only to be had by the mastery of the Cross which taketh away the self-wrapt guilt of the world.

With humility goes *patience* as a supreme confession of faith. Do not think that patience is a way of bearing trouble only. It is a way of doing work—especially the true secret of not doing too much work. It is a way of carrying success. It is not renouncing will and becoming careless. It is an act of will. It is a piece of manhood. To part with will is to become a *thing*. It is not mere resignation or indifference — which often goes with despair and not faith. It is a form of energy, even when it curbs energy. It is the Christian form of bravery, and it has the valour often to be called cowardice. It is the form of energy that converts suffering, and even helplessness, into action.

'I am ready not to do
At last, at last.'

It is the intense form of action which
made the power of the Cross, and
stamped the example of Christ in the
deepest way on the mind and heart
of the first Church.

Both humility and patience are
only Christian in the spirit of *thank-
fulness*.   Faith is for the Christian
enveloped in praise.   It is no gloomy
humility, no sombre patience, no dull
endurance, no resentful submission.
It is all clothed with hope.   It is the
faith and submission of a soul that
knows itself both immortal and redeemed, and owes all to God's purely
marvellous grace.   Its atmosphere is
glad hope.   Christian public worship
begins much more fitly with thanks-
giving than confession; it should open
as well as close with a doxology.   And

the central act of Christian worship
is the Eucharist—which is thanks-
giving. The spirit of Christian life
and worship is thanks and praise.
Whatever we offer to God, were it
life and health itself, is offered in the
name of Christ, in sequel to His Cross,
as the joyful response to our redemption there. You can never doubt,
when you actually see the thankful-
ness and sweetness in some life-long
martyrs and sufferers, that that is
the true Christian victory, whatever
the failures of their life may have
been. *There* is a perfection never
won by culture, art, or any success.

The next feature of perfection is
prayer—prayer as a habit, joy, and
prize of life. Humility takes the
form of reverence and yet communion. The heart converses with
God in Christ. It offers thanks, it
confesses sin, it makes its petitions,

but it above all converses with God.
That is the inmost energy of faith—
prayer. It is faith's habit of heart.
All *acts* of prayer become but expressions of this *habit.* Work goes
to this tune. Everything rises to
God's throne. Everything the child
does has a reference to the father,
direct or indirect. Every form of
prayer is speech with God the Father
and Redeemer. 'Praise is the speech
of faith, petition is the speech of
hope, intercession is the speech of
love, confession is the speech of
repentance.'

A further feature of Christian perfection is *duty.* Humility takes
shape as devotion to the will of God
in the natural and social order that
holds us. It is daily duty in our
relations and calling. If it is a
calling God cannot bless, it is not
for you. If He can bless it, it is a

contribution to Him.   And it is duty in the wide sense.   It is the duty, not of your business or family only, but of your social and civic position. Distrust the religion that makes you careless of social duties, public rights, and civic faithfulness.   How is society to be converted if conversion take men out of society?   How is the Kingdom to come if all the good are only 'saints,' if the 'saint' is a ruling caste among believers, and piety is more than faith?   A man's duty to the public does not justify him in neglecting his wife; but his duties to his family do not justify him in neglecting the public.   A man's religious duties are only partly met by the observances of his religion.   All the duties of his position are religious. And it is a perfection of another than the Christian kind that makes the Church the one field of God's perfect

will for him. That carries us back
to Romanism, and monkhood, and
the double morality of the religious
and the lay. What is called Church
work may be sacred enough; but it
is not in its nature more sacred than
the Christian's doing of the world's
work in his place and calling unto
God to Christ.

And the last feature of Christian
perfection is *love*, and especially love
to man. I have spoken of love to
God. That may be a passion. 'Thou
shalt love the Lord thy God with all
thy heart, soul, strength, and mind.'
But the love of man is less so. It is
at least less of an emotion than a
principle, and especially a principle
of action. 'Thou shalt love thy
neighbour as thyself.' But self-love
is not an emotion so much as a
principle, a habit of mind and action.
So with the love of men. When will

the public learn that that is not necessarily a tenderness of mood or manner? These have been lacking in some of the great lovers of their kind, and the dutiful assumption of them is a fertile source of Pharisaism. Love is not mere natural benevolence. It is not easy compliance. It does not consist in giving alms or gifts. Its type is rather the family love that grows up unmarked as a part of us than the passionate love of man and woman, which we fall into, and which seizes us with a mighty hand. It is a principle and habit of heart and conscience, a frame or temper of life which steadily desires the welfare of men, and especially their salvation, as if it were our own. It is anxious and considerate justice at least, especially in the public form. And it rises to be much more. Its desire is not to please but to bless. It can

be loud, and even sharp, when need-
ful, as well as kind and easily en-
treated. It shines through our
behaviour to men even when we seek
to do no more for them than is
involved in our daily calling. It
lurks in our words, our acts, our look,
our whole way of intercourse. It
does not always appear at first. It
comes home to you sometimes only
when you have known the man for
years; whereas the false thing takes
at the outset, and then wears thin.
It does not come and go with men's
behaviour. It is not easily offended.
It is fed from another source than
men's appreciation—at the Cross of
the misprized Christ. It is there
prepared for being misunderstood,
uncomprehended — and still going
on. When men have ceased to be
lovable for their own sake, it finds
a new Humanity welling up in

Christ, and keeping the heart sweet at that eternal spring.

It is this love that is the perfection of Christ. We do not really know Christ till we find it in Him and toward Him. It is inimitable in Him, yet communicable. It cannot be copied, but it can be conveyed. It cannot be presented to us, yet it can be learned. You cannot feel it in Him without its tending to make itself felt in you to others. You cannot trust His love and righteousness without gaining the disposition to trust love and justice above all things everywhere. Why do so few people in Christendom really trust love as the ruling power in mankind? Because Christ is not for them a real personality, loving and loved; because they have been taught to seek Christian perfection in the completeness of some institution, or the maintenance of some law, or the fever about some conviction. Something Christian is the object of their enthusiasm more than Christ. Something Christian more than Christ is the object of their faith. A conviction about Christ or His Church, held with great warmth, is not the love of Christ. Nor is it really the faith of Christ. These things are more the work of men than the free gift of God. And they cannot act on men as the free grace and love-charm of God only can. All these things belong to a lower stage of religion than Christ, to some kind of law religion, some kind of salvation by doing something, some kind of self-redemption or salvation by character or achievement. What we need is the personal impression of Christ, the personal sense of His cross, the fresh, renewing, vitalising,

K

sweetening contact of His soul in its wisdom, its tenderness, its action for us—and all so freely for us, so mercifully, so persistently, so thoroughly. What we need is the touch, the communion of that kind of perfection. We need to realise how in the Cross the defeat of that sort of goodness is really its victory, its ascent to the throne of the world. The Ruler of the world must be the consummation of the world. The Judge of *all* the earth must be the Law of all the earth. And the law of all must be the secret of all its harmony and perfection.

You must let that come home to *you*, to your own peculiar case. To be perfect with God you must have Christ come *home*, come HOME, to you and sit by your central fire—come home to *you*, to YOU, as if for the moment mankind were centred

in the burning point of your soul,
and you touched the burning point
of God's. You must court and haunt
His presence till it break forth on
you, and it become as impossible not
to believe as to believe is hard now.
Then we realise what we were made
for, made to be redeemed; we lay
hold by faith of our destiny of perfection in another; we are already in
spirit what it is latent in redemption
that we shall be—what some curse
in our nature seemed before to for-
bid and thwart our being. Our dry
rod blossoms. We put forth buds
one after another along the line of
life. We grow into a stately, seemly
tree, whose boughs are for shelter
and whose leaves are for healing.
Our pinched hearts expand, our
parched nature grows green. The
fever of life is cooled. Its fret is
soothed. Its powers stand to their

feet.   Its hopes live again.   Its charities grow rich.   We feel in that hour that this is what we were made for, and we are sure that we are greater than we know.   We find ourselves.   We lose our load.   We are delivered from our plague.   Our weakness is made strong.   Our enemies flee before us.   Our promised land is round us.   Life beckons where it used to appal.   And all things with us are returning through Christ, to the perfection of God from whom they came.

Edinburgh University Press
T. and A. CONSTABLE, Printers to His Majesty

Made in the USA
Monee, IL
13 January 2025

76721212R00090